About the Author

Samantha Novak is an audiobook narrator and author who lives in British Columbia with her husband.

The Sandman Chronicles
A Nocturnal Rhapsody

Samantha Novak

—

The Sandman Chronicles
A Nocturnal Rhapsody

Vanguard Press

VANGUARD PAPERBACK

© Copyright 2024
Samantha Novak

The right of Samantha Novak to be identified as author of this work has been asserted by her in accordance with the Copyright, Designs and Patents Act 1988.

All Rights Reserved

No reproduction, copy or transmission of this publication may be made without written permission.
No paragraph of this publication may be reproduced, copied or transmitted save with the written permission of the publisher, or in accordance with the provisions
of the Copyright Act 1956 (as amended).

Any person who commits any unauthorised act in relation to this publication may be liable to criminal prosecution and civil claims for damages.

A CIP catalogue record for this title is available from the British Library.

ISBN 978 1 78465 780 2

This is a work of fiction. Names, characters, businesses, places, events and incidents are either the product of the author's imagination or used in a fictitious manner. Any resemblance to actual persons, living or dead, or actual events is purely coincidental.

Vanguard Press is an imprint of
Pegasus Elliot Mackenzie Publishers Ltd.
www.pegasuspublishers.com

First Published in 2024

**Vanguard Press
Sheraton House Castle Park
Cambridge England**

Printed & Bound in Great Britain

For Jan Rios and Jerry Lesperance…
my dear friends on the other side.
I miss you terribly.

A battle for sleep has forever been the bane of my existence. If one doesn't obtain good sleeping habits when they're young, they're kissed with the insomniac's curse for life – like me. Trauma is usually the culprit, and everyone certainly has their own varying degrees of it.

Mine happened at four – an abduction-scenario that was a total misunderstanding, but because I'd gone through it alone, I was already scared silent by the time I had any opportunity to tell anyone about it. I swallowed the key to that secret the day I was returned home and forced myself to forget about the terror and abandonment, although its festering bubbles found ways to manifest in my experience of life. I was terrified to let myself be vulnerable and go to sleep at night. The nighttime was when the monsters came in my dreams, chasing me down, grabbing me, taking me away. I feared I wouldn't wake up. I feared someone was always after me. I didn't understand it fully, but I felt it, truly and greatly. I couldn't bear to sleep alone, so I grew up sleeping in my siblings' rooms. I became narcoleptic as a young adult and couldn't control when and where I slept. I got hit with sudden bouts of sleep paralysis, sometimes being completely awake mentally but physically unable to move my body even an inch. I tried to avoid sleeping, because I didn't want to deal with the nightmares anymore. Nightmares were supposed to be for children – why hadn't I outgrown them yet? They continued to haunt me and scream about an old trauma that happened so long ago – why should it even matter anymore? I just kept the key swallowed. I didn't even want to deal with it and what it could mean. So I took Xanax every night for eleven years to skip all the struggle, enjoying the convenience of slipping into a mini coma every night, where I didn't have to dream of anything, where I wasn't waking up constantly to the feeling that someone else was creeping in the corner of my room, where I could just rest without thinking about how to get it. *Swallow the pill, like the key, and forget the bullshit until morning.*

Eventually I realized that I couldn't live my whole life medicating myself to sleep every night. I knew that such a long-term habit would yield insufferable consequences at the proposal of detox. The withdrawal would force me to vomit up the key mentally and emotionally I'd swallowed at the beginning of my life and all the infantile bile that had been shoved down for so long with it. I knew it wouldn't be fun. I knew it would be painful. But I knew I had to do it.

In the middle of the night, when the withdrawal shakes were the worst, I found my hand reaching for a pen, as this poetic vomit spilled out of me onto the page. I didn't even have to think about it. The words flowed and expressed emotions from varying times of my life, that my swallowed key had kept hostage. These pages were what helped me get through something I didn't believe I could recover from. I was terrified that once I was freed of the comfort blanket that was my medication, I would return to exactly how I was struggling before when I was younger, and I wouldn't be able to function as an adult.

But I discovered the authentic catharsis that comes from writing about your deepest and most hidden feelings. I no longer felt weighed down by them. They weren't dirty little secrets within me anymore, but a tangible entity on the page. Captives finally set free.

Everything happens in baby steps. You can't possibly know the ways that you will heal and find success in your future during the times you are at your lowest. It's easier to condemn yourself to your fears than to have a blind faith in some miraculous outcome that doesn't seem within grasp. But you must find that faith if you truly want to heal. I was tired of my pain and suffering, and although I didn't know how I would ever feel better about my night life, I just kept living one night at a time.

Now, five years later, I have a completely different and updated view on who I am and my own pain. I don't suffer nearly as much as I used to, and I view all of my old traumas throughout my life as experiences that delivered valuable lessons and opportunities for growth and maturity. I am still plagued by violent nightmares, but now I view them through the lens of storytelling and find ways to turn them into stories. I found peace through developing and nurturing a deeper relationship with myself, through meditation, gratitude, reflection, art and writing – this book being a particularly prominent turning point in my life, which highlights a special moment of reunion, re-connection, healing and courage.

***

The cover image of this book is from a Sandman photo series I did with photographer, Miranda Steingraber, and model, Seth Nayes, at the Trans-Allegheny Lunatic Asylum in West Virginia, May 2014. It is one visual result of a two-day photo trip exploring the hauntingly empty halls and rooms of the largest hand-cut stone masonry building in the US (the second largest in the world).

Other artists have also contributed their art pieces that represent 'addiction', to add more presence and depth to this book, offering a visual look into the minds of those who know the suffering of the addict.

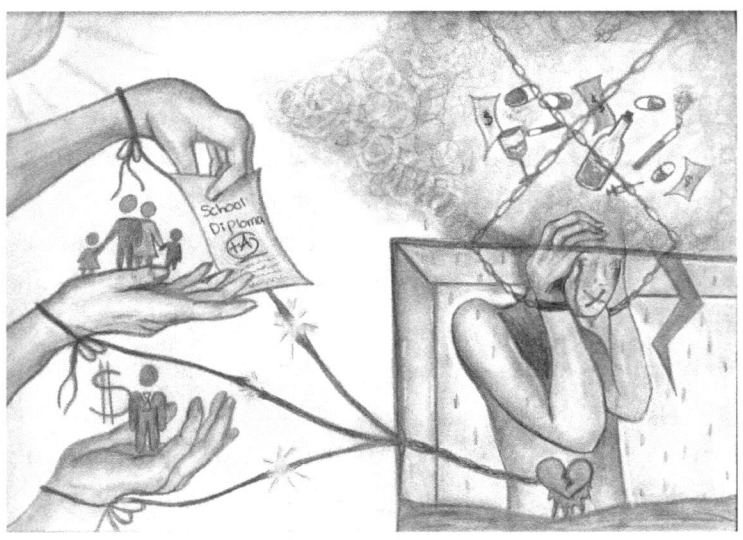

Artwork by Brooke Schnaebele

4.49 a.m.
The only thing I fear of your death
is the natural fading of the vividness of my memories
of your impact
your sweet voice
your beaming presence
the regularity of your friendship
your genuine loyalty
your unconditional love for me
because you may have been the actual first,
even beyond my parents and lovers,
to have really *known* the real me
and to love her better than anyone.
I fear to death the fading of these feelings
because you were the one who helped me learn to
love me.
You gave me the most important gift of all.
I only hope that I will honor you
in ways that prove your impact on my life
to let you know as you carry on your journey home
that I love you with every inch of my soul
and I thank you enormously for everything you are.

4.24 a.m.
Enslaved to my tomb
mummified lullaby
soaring astrally
to realms I can't always remember
living worship to my potions
oh, troubled souls who can't sit still
I rock my casket and it falls to the cold, stone floor
waking me violently every time
disrupting my treasures
unleashing the curse of the waking mummy
a repeated game of musical tombs
becoming a dance of its own;
whispers in candlelight.

3.40 a.m.
Broken waterfalls
parallel storylines
important conversations
all lurking right beneath the surface
my xanaxed memory fails me
of this alternative existence
a lingering hazy fog
that still poisons my mind
wiping the slate clean nightly
like it were an alien ritual
an abductee of my own doing
hoping to one day control
the craft of my hostaged heart.

1.36 a.m.
Enter this wild wood and view the haunts of nature.
Tonight I pierce the veil and sing out my celestial call,
summoning a visit from my Halloween Husband
who answers promptly to give me the sweetest ghost kiss
tingling on my mortal raspberry lips.

4.27 a.m.
Was I just dreaming of peril?
Echoed screams in the faint distance
yet when I wake it fogs over
like the rainclouds crying outside
pouring down secrets
teardrops of mystery
salty with suspense
the tear paths under my cerulean blues
are the evidence of probable cause
staining my bloodless cheeks
suggesting ominously
the perils of my detox dreams.

5.07 a.m.
Haunted souls fear the withdrawal shakes
internal imploding earthquakes
a bomb threat to my brain
igniting fuses of panic
threatening the repressed lava
beckoning to it like a skillful witch
testing her newfound powers
acid tingles like bubbly in my parched throat
spewing molten vomit for miles
aged like a fine French wine
pressed with indigo grapes
from the abduction vineyard
the palette unfamiliar to the tastes
of such hidden melancholy
that drips with childish terror
the acidity meeting the outside air for the first time
sizzles spontaneously
as the source of my cancerous wound
is finally exposed to the elements
serving as conduits for the transformational ritual
to heal this volcanic impasse.

3.51 a.m.
Wee hour wisdom
seeps through my scattered consciousness
pen to paper creating a vortex
where I become the mystery channel
not knowing what will transpire next
surface tensions or deep-seated memories
deciphering my almost-dreams like puzzle pieces
often denied the whole picture
but rather broken sentences to fill in the blanks
trying to make sense of my brain jumble
during the wee hours when
my spell wand takes the form of a pen
spelling out the secrets of my heart
penetrating the truth chamber
and extracting the precious cosmic serum
which flows like a swiftful river
down the pages of my night log
spiked with poetic flair
and teeming with guttural confessions
of my long-lost chapters
taunting to be read.

3.35 a.m.
Candied sugarplums and honey-glazed treasures
placebo trinkets pleasing to the eye
promising their own catalyst for relief
'Our sugars are the sweetest of all the lands'
soothing nectar like toddlers' sleeping dust
recipe ingredients from a witch's medicine cabinet
twinkles with presumed enchantment
the poisoned apple you take willingly
fantastical symbolism
alongside foreign incantations
creates the perfect formula for the bullshit pill
which may be able to fool the novice
yet is nothing but a midnight snack to the expert.

Artwork by Joanna Kanigua

4.46 a.m.
breaking glass shatters
the midnight casualty
of my equilibrium limbo
a slumbered dance done solo
weaving through the shadows
the professional sleepwalker;
a true Lady of the Night.

2.45 a.m.
The familiar earthquake battle ensues
weighted nothingness
stripped of my usual poisons
it feels like being forced to carry weights
even after your muscles surpass their point of exertion
a constant drain in the pit of my stomach
pulling me down like hypnotic quicksand
millions of serpents writhing underneath my skin
screaming for the missing chemical
too tired to write
too tired to sleep
eternally sick and tired of
this motherfucking warzone that is my mind.

4.02 a.m.
Hey, best friend
where have you gone to?
I try to find you everywhere
but your camo is so effective
it's hard to see you
I hope you're not lost
and blindly searching for your way
maybe you found a back door somewhere
and just outsmarted us all
crystalline distraction
but I still seek your tobacco aroma
or a visitation to my dreamworld
there are so many streets and places to hide there
that perhaps my landscapes are too confusing
and they've jumbled you up so you can't find me
but surely you weren't given a broken compass.
Oh, best friend
where have you gone to?
Blow your whistle please
so I can come find you.

2.35 a.m.
Damn you, demon noose
the infamous Hangman
your dull, drab decor bores me
that creaky swaying is so goddamn noisy
when they snuff out the flame
swinging back and forth like death monkeys
walking like Egyptians
headless in the desert
the galloping ghosts
of Zombie Ranch
ending the pain of one tortured soul
begins the torment of hundreds more
hanging from the suffocation rope
dreams and desires gone into dust;
another one lost to the mirage.

Artwork by Tamara Stockman

2.17 a.m.
Healing from my eleven-year flu
following synchronistic destiny clues
metallic chemical-coated pixie dust
the tiny blueberry pill casts line, hooks and sinkers
the metal pierces my cheek and I'm hooked
with a decade-long dependency
that couldn't possibly be drug addiction
if it came from a prescription pad
naive reasoning to candy-coat the abuse
of myself against the mirror monster
the vampiric pill that wipes my reflection
blindly supporting my benzo delusions
a willing victim caught in the web of entrapment
routinely slapping on my denial bandage
for the promised effects of symptom relief
a surface transaction that only grazes the issue at hand
which I accept during the years of my illness
until a new and better cure is available;
it already entices me like candy to a baby,
crack-cocaine for the broken ones.

2.38 a.m.
Can you feel the echo like me?
A secondary wave of sensation
that pierces and tickles and pinches my sensitive flesh
manipulative body tricks
appearing randomly like rainbows painted in the sky
each color emitting its own unique fragrance
which bites my memory bone in certain places
slapping me with phantom pains
that hit as quickly as tsunami winds
triggering my interpretation glands
which tune in and listen to the melting veil music
blaring like a celestial symphony
lyrical songs from spirit
a duet performance featuring my echoed touch
that sings the lost gospels of ethereal truth
the crescendoing church choir of my heart
penetrating the silence of the moments it interrupts
and returning to quiet as quickly as it began
haunting my temple with its lasting vibration
like the final piano key's resonating tone
echoing like my body does in the empty spirit church.

2.15 a.m.
unexplained abdominal pains
regretful wine pairings
pregnant with indigestive confusion
like a nervous kindergartner
gaseous sulfuric bubbles popping
in the pit of my unswallowable woes
cheesy acid souring my stomach
a newfound allergy making itself known
shedding my belly lining like a jeweled snakeskin.

2.48 a.m.
among the remains
discarded and still
she thought as she lay
she would remain there until
either they came to save her
or leave her to be killed
by the vultures who watched her
for the sake of the thrill.

1.53 a.m.
phantom vanilla
breezes in to say hello
the sweet smell of deja vu
tickles my whiskers
curly q lips.

3.45 a.m.
You are warm winter rain
the protective cloak that surrounds me
your fingers on my scalp; methodical comfort man
hypnotic whispers adorned with angel wings
gently encouraging me to fly
above the smoggy clouds of structured thought
piercing the skies of sweet clarity
swimming across Heaven's ocean
following the path of pastel corral
white sand diamonds glittering in the sun
where an icy crystal throne awaits
new vantage points colorfully displayed on the horizon
your loving whispers told me to study these sights
fearlessly roaring with everything I am
melding as one with the clarity I seek
I finally become Me
divine reunion;
hope sparkles in the distance.

1.14 a.m.
dried up well of sorrow
the tears have all turned into rain
flying away from this wretched place
to kiss the clouds like they've always dreamed
marshmallow fluff
that turns them into raspberry lemonade
showering sweetness across the countryside
nature's love nectar
necessary nutrients for the masses
originating from the pain rain;
my chrysalis of hope.

2.15 a.m.
Four-year-old fingers wrapped around my neck
melting into me like liquid fright
hypochondriac pinwheels between my pigtails
giant bloody chickens and cartoony monsters taunt
me
I hate the closet ghost lights
the man under my bed won't let me sleep
stay tuned for the midnight parade
the sleepwalker's special
keep your distance or get stabbed in the neck
like me from all those lives ago
I still remember the man who killed me
what does it mean?
My elementary logic can't quite explain
and so every night I've been afraid
believing I'll drop dead as soon as the light fades
always on the precipice of being snuffed out like a
candle flame
Will I die or will I wake?
Am I crazy or am I sane?
Will I ever be better than yesterday?
Or have I been sentenced to eternal pain?

1.25 a.m.
I probably drive him mad
every night channeling the Cheshire Cat
gab, gab, gab, gab, gab
whimsical nonsense mad, mad, mad
the hookah smoke spells identity crises
smells
rosemary, lavender, cinnamon, grape
how much more madness may my merry mind make
car goes buh-bye, man does rape
silly me, silly me; let's celebrate!
Only I can bake the rape cake.

Where did he go? Where did he go?
Oh, surfer boy in your curls?
I baked you a cake, I baked you a cake
made of porn, champagne, diamonds and pearls
Oh no, did you say? Oh no, did you say?
Shut up surfer boy, sit the fuck down
I don't care you're not hungry, you'll eat the whole thing
turn that motherfucking frown upside down
Did I make you cry, son?
Say what, you can't move?
Don't worry Joshy Poo, you'll move when I'm through

This cake has been frozen for seven long years
made on Hollywood Boulevard from fear-frozen
tears
salty and sweet, a mouth-watering treat
a dream come true for a creep like you.

I figured as one last courtesy
I'd feed you this cake personally
make sure you wipe the plate clean
we both know how messy you can be
but you know there is this one last thing
Surfer boy, pay attention honey
I'm shoving this rape cake back down your throat
a pie in the face is always funny.

3.36 a.m.
I so wish I could sleep through the night
I long for uninterrupted, peaceful slumber
a calm and relaxed body and mind
oblivious to the world around me
snoring gingerly in contentment
a peace of mind so serene
I wake effortlessly in the morning light
blissfully devoid of late-night rendezvous'
having ended the long affair with my anxious mind.
I miss my wonder drug.

3.45 a.m.
Lunar Lady
looking luminescent
silver explosion
incandescent
aluminum rays
beaming moondust essence
a sun-spun toast
to your evanescence.

Artwork by Karrie Alshehry Amore

4.17 a.m.
So tired of these mid-sleep wakening's
I don't even want to write this damn book anymore
burn the pages like a Salem diary
to turn my pain into flames

I let go and banish them all to Hell
to cremate the afflicted carcasses
incinerate the hate
crucify the tormented misery
singing praises to the burning blasphemy
my heart searches desperately for signs of peace in the void
but the warpath is nothing but scorched terrain
a scabbed scar as a lasting reminder
of the melancholic narrative that is my nightlife.

2.17 a.m.
New tactics are clearly required
fake it til I make it and don't say I can't
think of things that make me inspired
cry if I need to, scream, vent and rant
what no longer serves me I cast to the fire
singing praises as I twirl and dance
saying no to my fears and yes to my desires
making moves to seduce the Sandman.

4.13 a.m.
How we meet again, my 4 a.m. friend
pleasure to make your acquaintance
maybe our visits aren't all that bad
rebound insomnia testing my patience
expected phenomena of the clockwork habit
wakes me with its toasty fragrance
enticing me to raise my witching-hour pen
this nocturnal rhapsody is contagious.

5.07 a.m.
Twinkling twilight sparkles in the windowsill
the sound of rain is music to my ears
my darling lover snoring contently next to me
these past weeks coated his lips with my tears
Khalifa Kush, my bedside friend
helping me melt these infantile fears
rewiring my brain to love the way
I've battled my demons after all these years.